CARPEDIA'S
52 LESSONS LEARNED

A collection of insights
learned from experience

Peter Follows
Carpedia International Ltd.

RESULTS NOT REPORTS®

ISBN: 978-0-9881505-1-5

Edited by Julie Packard
Artwork - See Image Credits, page 110.

For information: www.carpedia.com

First edition
Published and printed in Canada

Library and Archives Canada registration,
book layout and production management
through the TRI Publishing™ program
TRIMATRIX Management Consulting Inc.
www.trimatrixmanagement.com

CONTENTS

LESSONS LEARNED #		PAGE
	LESSONS LEARNED DEFINED	5
1	NUMBERS LIE	6
2	DON'T PUT DOWN YOUR AUDIENCE	8
3	WRENCH TIME: THE SECRET TO PERFORMANCE IMPROVEMENT	10
4	CLIENTS DON'T CARE WHAT CONSULTANTS THINK	12
5	THE LEAST MANAGED PART OF A BUSINESS	14
6	TO CHANGE BEHAVIOR, CHANGE THE CONSEQUENCES	16
7	BENCHMARKING OTHERS RARELY HELPS	18
8	TOO MANY REPORTS, TOO LITTLE TIME	20
9	INNOVATE THE PRODUCT, ENERGIZE THE ORGANIZATION	22
10	THE KEY TO CONTINUOUS IMPROVEMENT	24
11	WHAT YOU SAY, WHAT THEY HEAR	26
12	AVOID EMPTY JARGON	28
13	WHY WALL MAPS TRUMP POWERPOINT DECKS	30
14	THE BLACK BOX OF SCHEDULING	32
15	THE PROBLEM WITH CORPORATE POOL TABLES	34
16	OBSERVATIONS: THE MOST USEFUL TOOL THAT MANAGER'S DON'T USE	36
17	A STRATEGY NEEDS TO SOLVE A PROBLEM	38
18	TO IMPROVE PRODUCTIVITY, IMPROVE MANAGEMENT	40
19	THE HIDDEN COST OF A BRIEFCASE FULL OF MONEY	42
20	START WITH THE CONCLUSION	44
21	LOST IN TRANSLATION	46
22	WHAT DO YOU MEAN BY A "GOOD" DAY?	48
23	EVERY MANAGER'S ABOVE AVERAGE	50
24	TOO MANY GOOD IDEAS	52
25	DON'T ASK FOR FEEDBACK IF YOU DON'T WANT IT	54
26	BE CAREFUL OF STOPE RATS	56

CONTENTS

LESSONS LEARNED #		PAGE
27	ATTACK THE RED TIME FIRST	58
28	WHAT DOES "IMPLEMENTATION" MEAN ANYWAY?	60
29	NOBODY GETS THEIR MBA TO BE A SALES PERSON	62
30	THE PROBLEM WITH INDUSTRY EXPERTS	64
31	ADDITION IS EASIER THAN SUBTRACTION	66
32	DON'T SEND BACK THE HEINEKEN	68
33	THE UNFORTUNATE HABIT OF ANSWERING QUESTIONS TOO QUICKLY	70
34	DON'T FEED THE PIGS	72
35	WHAT DO YOU DO WITH A "VARIANCE"?	74
36	DON'T FORGET THE ACTUAL WORKERS	76
37	THE DANGER OF ASSUMPTIONS	78
38	NEVER PRESENT "NEW" IDEAS	80
39	THE INTRODUCTION SETS THE TONE	82
40	YOU CAN'T ASSESS YOUR OWN WORKLOAD	84
41	ALWAYS NEGOTIATE PRICE LAST	86
42	HOW TO MAKE INTERNAL PERFORMANCE IMPROVEMENT GROUPS SUCCEED	88
43	WHAT'S THE REAL PROBLEM?	90
44	OPERATIONS HAS TO OWN THE PROJECT	92
45	TWO WAYS TO IMPROVE PRODUCTIVITY IN VARIABLE ENVIRONMENTS	94
46	ACTUALLY, YOU DO NEED TO REINVENT THE WHEEL	96
47	THE OFFICE CAN LEARN FROM THE PLANT FLOOR	98
48	THE MISCONCEPTION ABOUT EMPLOYEE EMPOWERMENT	100
49	THE MOST DANGEROUS KIND OF RESISTANCE	102
50	THE EMOTIONAL ROLLER COASTER	104
51	IT'S EASY TO LOSE SIGHT OF THE PURPOSE	106
52	LEARNING THROUGH OBSERVATION	108
	IMAGE CREDITS	110
	ABOUT CARPEDIA INTERNATIONAL	112

LESSONS LEARNED DEFINED

This book is a collection of the things we have learned, mostly from our clients, over the past 20 years. Many of the lessons discussed were learned after we made an error or did something that would later prove unwise. Sometimes, our clients or close business associates advised us against doing something, but we went ahead and did it anyway. So this short collection is not a celebration of Carpedia's collective brilliance. It is more a humble retelling of how we have learned some very important lessons, all of which have shaped the culture of our company and the methods we use.

We wrote this book because it seemed to us to be an interesting way to present some very useful information, which we had not known, for one reason or another. Our approach goes against the conventional grain, where the management consultant is the teacher and the client is the student – although we've never truly bought into that archetype. In our experience, the work we do with our clients is very much a mutual journey of discovery – of trying to figure out better ways to do things. Along the way, we've learned that not everything that looks great on paper actually works, so we always try to learn from our errors and start again. The creativity and humility this requires are what actually make our line of work engaging over time. And they are a rich source for this collection of stories.

Not all the lessons learned were intuitive. Some were a little surprising, and some were the kind of thing you only learn through experience. We believe that they will prove useful to today's managers, as they deal with the neverending challenges of trying to improve the performance of their organizations.

We hope you find *Carpedia's 52 Lessons Learned* insightful and helpful to both you and your organization – especially considering the moments of dismay and humiliation we endured while learning them in the first place!

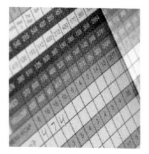

NUMBERS LIE

In many organizations, some of the reported performance numbers aren't very "real." It's very similar to people's golf handicaps. The handicap system is a wonderful mechanism to track performance and let you know where you stand. But it is most useful if you count all your strokes and play by golf's stringent rules. Many golfers, some more often than others, stray from those rules and artificially inflate their performance.

Companies do this as well. These performance numbers are often inaccurate:

- Labor productivity
- Inventory accuracy
- Schedule attainment
- Lead times

There are reasons for these inaccuracies in every case. Productivity may be high because current performance is measured against inflated standards. Inventory numbers are often inaccurate due to the way companies cycle count. Schedule attainment is frequently wrong because it is based on volume and not on the product or services actually scheduled. Measured lead times often omit certain steps.

So why do organizations do this? It may be for the same reasons that some golfers inflate their handicap: it looks better, it feels better, it's easier, and it seems relatively harmless. The argument often used in business is the actual numbers don't matter: only the trend is important. But this isn't true, if you really want to improve.

Improvement and innovation only come when there is a gap between where you are and where you want to be. The more you inflate your current performance, the smaller the gap. The smaller the gap, the less motivation there is to close it. It's one of the reasons companies started benchmarking other companies: to show managers that performance gaps existed.

So a healthy skepticism is important when looking at performance numbers. If you really seek innovation and continuous improvement, you need to review the way you measure performance and evaluate it from a zero base whenever you can.

DON'T PUT DOWN
YOUR AUDIENCE

We had done quite a lot of work in the trucking industry and, through word of mouth, were invited to speak at a national convention. We prepared an insightful speech that criticized the industry for its lack of innovation, among other things. In advance of the convention we shared the presentation with one of our business advisors, who happened to be a well regarded CEO in the very industry we were addressing. He listened quietly. Then, when we were finished, he laughed and said, "You've got to be joking!"

Not really intending the speech to be funny, we asked him what he meant. He said, "Guys, you're talking to people who have successfully built their own businesses, who have paid money to come to a national convention to have fun and maybe learn a few new things. They didn't come to be lectured by consultants. And resist the urge to question them, because you will be asking them to put themselves down, which they obviously won't want to do."

We thanked him for the input and ignored it.

At the convention, we somewhat ironically followed a motivational speaker, who we were convinced would bomb. We were wrong about that too. By the end of the presentation, the mood in the room was electric. He had people shouting and jumping out of their chairs, and there was a feverish buzz in the air. We were almost trampled as people exiting the room scrambled to buy copies of his books and DVDs.

We walked onstage and immediately the person who was introducing us mispronounced our company name – another lesson learned. We then started into our academic criticism of the industry, hoping to ride the wave of the enthusiasm from the previous talk. Talk about throwing water on a fire! With each point we made about how the profit of the industry was declining because of a lack of differentiation, you could actually feel the excitement of the previous speech drain from the room. To prove our case, we put a convoluted value proposition up on the screen, ripped straight from the industry leader's web pages, and asked someone from the audience to comment on it. He politely refused twice. Finally, after the third prodding, he explained, "Look, I work for the company you're using as an example, so it isn't appropriate for me to comment." The awkwardness that followed may be the only thing that anyone remembers from that presentation (including us).

So we learned that if you are ever speaking to a group of people, by all means illuminate, inspire or entertain, but don't put them down to make your point.

WRENCH TIME:
THE SECRET TO
PERFORMANCE IMPROVEMENT

Early in his career, one of our partners asked an experienced consultant what to look for when working in a maintenance area. The veteran said, "The same thing you look for in every area: wrench time." He went on to explain that the business world is full of people with titles. Their titles represent the special skills they have learned, but they they may not actually use those skills enough: salespeople who don't spend much time selling; managers who don't spend much time managing; and mechanics who don't spend much time with a wrench in their hands – or what he referred to as "wrench time." He said the secret to performance improvement is to figure out how to increase wrench time, no matter what the functional area.

This turned out to be a key insight and a very helpful way to think about how to improve any functional area. It's often surprising when we calculate how much time people actually spend at their core task. When we work with companies, we analyze this distribution of time. It's not uncommon for us to observe the following:

- Mechanics spend less than 10% of their time physically doing maintenance (e.g., turning a wrench on a piece of equipment).
- Sales reps spend less than 15% of their time advancing a sale.
- Managers spend less than 5% of their day actively managing others.

The task for a consultant or manager is to identify the obstacles that prevent the person from using their core skill more frequently throughout the course of the day. A mechanic may lose a lot of potential wrench time waiting for assignments; by not having the right supplies on hand; or traveling around the plant or building. Different assignment methods, tool preparation or layout changes could free up valuable wrench time. A salesperson may simply not have enough leads. Or he or she may spend too much time on administration or traveling to meetings. Managers often spend little time actively managing their staff because they lack effective scheduling and follow-up tools and spend too much time fire-fighting. In every case, if you can figure out how to free up or capture time and convert it into wrench time, performance will improve.

CLIENTS DON'T CARE WHAT CONSULTANTS THINK

One of the key things clients expect in a performance improvement project is that their managers will take ownership of the changes that are required to improve performance. This is not always an easy thing to do, because often not all managers have bought into the need to change.

There are a number of steps in our methodology that are designed to help managers take ownership of a project. One of the best came to us from a senior executive at a division of H.J. Heinz.

As we approach the halfway point of a project, we have a key meeting that we call the "focus meeting." As the name implies, it is designed to focus both us and the managers who are working with us. Often there are many good ideas for change, but we have to pare them down into specific things that can be accomplished in a reasonable time frame. The focus meeting is a fairly big deal, where the current state is presented and critiqued, and the changes required to get to a better state are visually displayed.

For years we would work through the night to create these big displays. Then our consultants would present them to senior executives, while the managers looked on. One year, the day before the focus meeting, we dropped in to see the senior executive who had hired us and gave him a quick overview of what to expect the next day.

After we finished, he said, "It sounds great, but I don't want you presenting this to me. I don't really care what you think. I only care about what my managers think. I'd like them to present tomorrow." We mumbled something like, "Of course," and left the room, trying not to let the client see the panic in our eyes. It quickly dawned on us that he was right, and our approach was wrong. It wasn't important what we thought. The only thing that mattered was whether or not managers believed they could improve.

We worried that we hadn't properly engaged the managers to the point where they would be comfortable presenting their ideas to their boss. Fortunately we were working with very strong managers who embraced the chance to speak for themselves, and the meeting was successful.

From that project forward, client managers always present the focus meeting, and we say very little unless asked. The experience forced us to re-engineer the front end of our projects to ensure that managers are properly engaged from the opening meetings.

THE LEAST MANAGED PART OF A BUSINESS

One of the more intriguing things we've learned while working across industries and functional areas is that the actual point where work physically gets done – what we call the "point of execution" – is the least managed part of a business or organization. Managers spend a lot of time planning what needs to happen and then reporting on what did happen, but not much time managing the point where things actually happen.

The biggest problem with this approach is that things always happen that are not in the plan (e.g., information is missing, machines aren't available, etc.). It may not be obvious because employees don't stop working: they work around or bandage the problem as best they can, or they move on and do something else. So managers often don't see or know about these problems. The problems become accepted by employees as part of the workday. Reporting is often too long after the fact, the result being that recurring problems eventually are just built into the plan, further obscuring them from management.

So why don't managers spend more time at the point of execution? One of the main reasons is that managers often don't like following up on their staff. Often managers and employees are not comfortable with the concept of "following up." (This is particularly true in office environments and especially in professional areas, such as engineering). Both managers and employees misinterpret the purpose of following up and often wrongly label it "micro-management."

The real purpose of following up is for the manager to see how well the area or individual is achieving what was planned. This is very important in order to co-ordinate all the moving parts that exist in any business or organization. Following up in real time allows the manager to identify problems as they occur and make changes to get back on plan. It is not to police employees or to micro-manage them.

In order to follow up effectively, a well-thought-out schedule needs to be in place that outlines where the employee should be through the day or week – not simply a sequence of activities or "hot list" of things to do.

So while planning and reporting are important functions of good management, much can be gained by improving how work is scheduled and by making sure the manager helps remove obstacles that interfere with the flow of work. We know, from experience, that if you can get to the point where the followup is meaningful and helpful for employees, both managers and employees will adopt the routine and enjoy working together to get things accomplished.

TO CHANGE THE BEHAVIOR, CHANGE THE CONSEQUENCES

Early in our company's history, we decided to be an "implementation" firm, rather than a typical "consulting" firm. We did this because in order to sell anything we had to demonstrate a financial return for our services, because nobody knew who we were and therefore weren't inclined to pay us merely for advice. This decision has had lasting implications for how we work and what we focus on. In many ways, it has brought us closer to understanding how truly difficult it is to be a manager or to get people to change their behaviors. While we don't pretend to be clinical experts in the study of human behavior, in 20 years of observation we've learned a few things that may be helpful for managers dealing with behavior change[1]. One of the most important lessons we have learned is that you don't change people's behavior simply by telling them to do something different: you have to change or reshape the consequences that occur when they do things.

We think of behavior in three parts: there is some kind of directive or guideline; then there is the actual behavior; and finally there are consequences for doing what was directed (or for not doing what was directed). The consequences, positive or negative or neutral, reinforce whatever behavior was observed. To change someone's behavior, you usually need to reshape the environment and modify the consequences. Managers try to do this all the time, particularly using compensation arrangements and incentives. The trouble with relying on compensation to drive behavior is that it only works if the person sees a direct correlation between the incentive reward and the behavior. The further the consequence is from the direct behavior, the less influence it has.

Another mistake is to assume that the person can, in fact, control the behavior. Often we find it is the environment that causes people to do things. An employee completes a customer's order by including items that were planned for a later order. The negative consequences of missing the first order are more immediate and certain than the future consequences of potentially missing a later order. He may have no way of ensuring that all items are ready when needed. Even more confusing, he may be celebrated for getting the order out on time – a positive reinforcement of the wrong behavior.

Of all the areas where we work, behavior is the hardest to analyze and change. It's helpful if you take something nebulous like "behavior" and make it more specific. A behavior must be something you can count and measure, such as a salesperson cancelling meetings. A behavior is not something vague, such an attitude (e.g., being arrogant). If you can measure the behavior, then you can study it and you can try to understand what drives the behavior. Fortunately there are studies and techniques that can help you do this. The key, however, is to focus on the consequences and see if you can modify the environment or the actual consequences themselves.

[1] *For a more advanced discussion and analysis on human behavior, see* Science and Human Behavior *by B. F. Skinner*

BENCHMARKING OTHERS RARELY HELPS

The idea of benchmarking your processes against other divisions, firms or industries to drive innovation or develop new performance targets has long been appealing. Unfortunately, we have learned that it can be very costly, and it just doesn't work very well in practice. Trying to benchmark a company's processes against other companies (or even divisions) presents three basic problems. (1) It's very difficult to define the parameters of a process carefully enough so that you can actually make meaningful comparisons. (2) Processes never operate in isolation. To study them, you also need to look at the corresponding management systems and organizational behaviors. And (3) because of problems 1 and 2, it can be a very expensive and time-consuming exercise to do properly.

Perhaps the biggest issue is that even if you do overcome the problems mentioned above, managers, who ultimately determine whether the benchmarking information is useful or not, have a tendency to agree with positive variances and dismiss negative ones. Favorable variances reinforce current practices and can actually create complacency. Negative variances can be all too easily challenged, because the business environments being compared are inevitably different in some way. It's often too easy for managers to use different cultures, systems, people, customers and facilities to diminish the validity of a benchmarking exercise. Very often the last comment you hear is the inevitable "apples and oranges" analogy.

Some businesses use benchmarking to inspire and energize their managers – almost like a form of industrial tourism. This may be perfectly valid and certainly gives managers a chance to see how others tackle certain common issues. We actually use a form of benchmarking extensively on projects, but we only benchmark processes against themselves. We will look at a process and see how well it has been accomplished in the past. This creates a "best demonstrated" benchmark against which we can measure and study the reasons for variances. If we (and the area managers) can figure out what helped create the "best demonstrated" performance, then we can try to recreate those circumstances or conditions on a more regular basis. The advantage of this approach is that managers are striving to replicate something they have already achieved with their own cultures, systems, people, customers and facilities.

TOO MANY REPORTS, TOO LITTLE TIME

When we work for an organization, we always look closely at how managers plan, execute that plan, and then report on the results. We've learned over time that the one area where there is never a shortage of information is in the reporting. Planning can be hit and miss; execution is often ad hoc or missing (as we've discussed before); but there is rarely a shortage of reports. In many cases there are too many reports.

We aren't sure why this is the case, but we suspect it is because it's much easier to create a report than it is to eliminate a report. Many new managers will create or modify a report for their own purposes, but they are reluctant to kill off existing reports for fear that someone, somewhere, might need the information. Distribution lists are often quite wide, and sometimes there are a few pieces of information on each report that could be useful, so it's ultimately easier to simply add to the pile. Sometimes it's also easier to build a new report than to navigate a request through the

IT work queue. Over time this creates an obvious problem, as there is simply too much information.

We see a few key common problems with reports:

- Many reports are "status" reports. They tell a manager the current status of something, but they aren't very effective in convincing the manager to do anything about it. This is often the case when managers are copied on a distribution list, but don't really need the information to do their own job effectively.

- Many reports are too late and after the fact. Managers are very busy people. The longer it takes to get information to them, the less useful the information. It's simply hard to backtrack when there are new and present problems and issues that need attention.

- Many reports contain too much information. Reports often don't "cut to the chase" quick enough and really focus on the few key indicators that a manager is supposed to manage. Ideally a report highlights a variance to a plan of some kind. The value to the manager is that the variance provides a focus for problem-solving. If the plan isn't solid or bought into, then the variance loses its usefulness and doesn't trigger any response or action on the part of the manager.

A manager's time is a valuable commodity in any business or organization. Reports can be very time-consuming and, as discussed, they can cause a lot of valuable time to be wasted or at least used ineffectively. It's worthwhile to periodically review the value of the reports that are generated. In our experience, most businesses usually need fewer, more focused and more timely reports. The benefit for managers is that this reduces clutter, frees up time, and makes the reporting far more useful.

INNOVATE THE PRODUCT, ENERGIZE THE ORGANIZATION

One of our clients was the COO of a large international container-shipping company. He'd made a name for himself by taking over newly acquired companies and making them more successful – no small feat when you consider how common it is for acquisitions to fail. One of our partners had worked with him over a number of years and was fascinated by what appeared to be a formula for his success. So he asked the client if he, in fact, had a methodology. Our client answered rather matter of factly, "Yes. We call it 'product innovation.' You have to improve the product in a meaningful way."

The reason, he explained, is that by focusing on the product, they were forced to really understand what customers wanted most; how well the company delivered those things; and how the company differentiated itself from competitors. If they could figure out how to tweak the product (or in this case service) and make it better, there were a number of key benefits:

- This gave the company's salesforce new inspiration and a reason to sell. It also gave customers and prospects a reason to take a sales meeting.
- It gave the company a fresh platform to market their service offering.
- It also provided a reason to market internally and energize the employees.

He hired us a few times to speak to his customers and to compare his company's performance against competitors' on key attributes that influence customers' buying decisions, as well as to determine how easy or difficult it would be for customers to switch suppliers. From this information he would examine which attributes were important but not "owned" by any single competitor. He'd then see if they could modify their service to capture and own that particular attribute, and then build the company's delivery and marketing around it.

Obviously this is a little trickier to do in practice than it is to write about it, but the underlying concept is very useful. If you can figure out an underserviced attribute that is important to your customers, and you can modify what you do to "own" that attribute in the mind of your customers, you can create a powerful competitive position, as well as energize your organization.

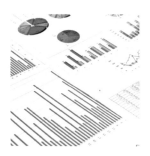

THE KEY TO CONTINUOUS IMPROVEMENT

During a project for H.J. Heinz, we worked with a very bright client who taught us a great deal about managing variances – and why this is so important for continuous improvement. He did it in a fairly combative way: he threatened to shut down the project. He told us that if we published production schedule "targets" on the area performance visibility boards, he would march us out the door.

His logic was insightful: "Leave the averages for the people who look at averages. How am I supposed to instill a culture of continuous improvement if my managers are not measuring 100% of the variation?" He continued, "It is the responsibility of the leads and supervisors to understand all the variation, not just the variation to a target. A target is just some average that we made up with spreadsheets."

To explain this: all schedules or plans have some variances built into them, because it is virtually impossible to operate without occasional problems. So you may plan to perform at 90% of what you are capable of doing (without any problems). If a manager uses the 90% as a base and performs at 85%, he or she will account for a 5% variance, when in fact there is actually a 15% variance.

It was an epiphany for the project team and contributed to an extraordinarily successful project. One of the many obstacles that we needed to overcome was the reality that areas would rarely hit "perfection," which might lead to lower morale. Through hard work on communication and leadership development, the local managers were able to coach and show their operators that success at the point of execution was identifying the waste – not achieving 100%. This understanding also helped define and clarify the role of the leads, supervisors and managers: waste reduction was their priority, and they had to work together.

When we began the engagement, the factory ran with 40% waste in the process. We finished the project at 30%. Five years later, we were invited back to the same factory with a new mandate. They had managed to reduce waste further to 20% but needed some help to break through to 15%. It may be the best example of continuous improvement we have ever seen. They kept improving in part because of the drive of the client and the skill of the people, but in large part because they refused to manage to an average.

WHAT YOU SAY, WHAY THEY HEAR

In some ways this lesson was learned similarly to Lessons Learned #2: "Don't Put Down Your Audience," when we inexplicably chose a national trucking convention to criticize the trucking industry. When you are talking to a group of people, it is very important to understand and appreciate their sensitivity to what you are saying, because what you mean and what people hear can be very different things.

Each summer we hold a company event over a couple of days. It's a good way to get all our frequent flyers together, and we use the occasion to hold a three-hour company update meeting sometime on the first day. At one particular meeting, we spent the entire time going through tremendous detail about our positioning, performance and people strategies. Despite three long hours of presentation, all that people remembered (and, in fact, still remember to this day) is when the president of the company said, "The core of our people strategy this year is to improve our recruiting."

What he meant was that people are, of course, critical to a consulting firm, and it is a good idea to try to improve how you can attract the best candidates. What people heard was: "We need to improve the quality of our people" (meaning "find better staff than all of you here").

It was a fairly innocent comment but it caused a surprising amount of internal turmoil. It also caused any other key points from the meeting to be lost. The lesson we learned was to think through carefully what you say to a group and try to understand how your words will be interpreted. It also reinforced the importance of rehearsing presentations in advance. Sometimes you need others to listen to your words because it is not easy to interpret your own words other than the way you intended. But when your job is to communicate ideas, which is a key responsibility of all managers, it is important that what you say and what people hear are the same thing.

AVOID
EMPTY JARGON

In the early days of the company, our founders had to figure out how to position the firm in the consulting market. They came from both strategy and operational backgrounds, and from their experience they felt there was an opening for a strategically oriented implementation firm. They believed that existing strategy consultants didn't implement their ideas very well, and that productivity consultants were too focused on labor cost and not on total business profitability.

So they came up with what they thought was a brilliant slogan: "Strategic Productivity."

They told one of their clients, a CEO of a fairly large transportation conglomerate, the slogan, explained its meaning and then waited for his response. He thought about it for about two seconds and said, "I think you guys have taken two over-used words and created a meaningless phrase."

He added some useful advice: "Avoid jargon. It doesn't mean anything to anybody. If something can be explained in a multitude of ways, it doesn't mean anything. I could come up with five definitions of 'strategic productivity.' It just sounds like you are trying to impress someone. Think about what makes you appealing to potential clients, and come up with a very simple slogan that says what you mean." Thanking the CEO somewhat bitterly for the advice, the founders went back to the drawing board and eventually came up with the slogan that continues today as the company's registered trademark: "Results Not Reports."

The lesson learned was a powerful one and became part of the culture of the company. Any use of jargon in presentations or even casual discussions is frowned upon, which, not surprisingly, is universally appreciated by clients at all levels.

WHY WALL MAPS TRUMP POWERPOINT DECKS

We are well known by our clients for our large wall-map presentations. Before the digital revolution these maps were extremely cumbersome to put together. Newly minted MBAs, brought on board, eager to flex their management acumen, would be taught how to cut and paste charts and images on large strips of bristol board. Understandably, a few questioned why this wasn't mentioned in the interview process.

As the digital world took hold, PowerPoint presentations became very popular. Even clients started to question whether these massive wall charts were not a little out of step with modern capabilities. So we adapted and tried doing our presentations with cutting-edge slide shows. In the process we learned a couple of interesting things:

- Too much color and fancy slide transitions may look great, but they are distracting to the message.
- Three-dimensional charts are clever, but difficult to read and

understand.

However, the most important thing we learned is that once a slide is presented, it disappears. Then another slide is presented and it too disappears. After a while, people forget what was presented beforehand, and the continuity of the message disappears. The real power of the giant wall map was that it kept all the key points front and center, and people could easily scan back to review previous points. This allowed them to make the connections that are often so important to fully understanding how you get from A to B. It also stopped the endless debate of whether or not to hand out the slide deck before the presentation. If you did hand it out, people would invariably jump ahead and pay less attention to what you were saying. If you didn't hand it out, people would be slightly irritated that you were holding back information and sometimes felt they were being manipulated. With the wall map, everything was already in full view. You just needed to explain it.

In a change-management process, understanding the connections between what you are going to change (process), how you are going to manage the new processes (management systems), and what you need to do differently (behavior) are critical. So we went back to using the wall maps, although they are now digital and we hear fewer complaints from our new hires. We learned to use digital technology to support the method, rather than change the method to fit the technology.

THE BLACK BOX OF SCHEDULING

Over the years we have learned that scheduling is one of the most important and least understood aspects of many organizations, possibly because it's generally so dull a subject. If you start talking about planning parameters and standards, you'll also see most people's eyes get heavy. We often joke that our MBA recruits always want to talk about strategy and finance. Nobody ever went to business school to become a production scheduler. But every industry we have entered has been marked by top clients teaching us how important scheduling is for them to manage profitability, and for us us in turn when working with their management to try to figure out how to improve it. Here are a few of the many interesting locations and situations where we have had to figure out how to schedule more effectively:

- Operating rooms: to optimize the use of physicians' time.
- MRI diagnostic equipment: to manage wait lists.
- Aircraft assembly lines: to match inventory with production flow.
- Restaurant kitchens and wait staff: to match meal patterns.

- Retail store personnel: to balance the ebb and flow of shoppers.
- Housekeeping staff: to co-ordinate with hotel room availability.
- Truck delivery stops: to optimize loads and frequencies.
- Software engineering milestones.
- Sales call patterns: to optimize customer value and requirements.
- Procurement part reviews: to drive material savings through alternate sourcing.

In every industry, scheduling the resources to match demand is the key to success. It very often makes the difference between high- and low-performing organizations. Yet despite its significance, it's also remarkable how often there is a black-box methodology when it comes to scheduling. It's often strangely difficult to analytically determine how exactly scheduling is accomplished. When we dig into the details, we often discover some of the following:

- Sales forecasts aren't trusted, so operations people create their own.
- Schedules change frequently, making control of inventory requirements extremely difficult.
- Planning standards are inconsistent, not used, or considered inaccurate.
- The ERP system used by the organization does not generate actual schedules, only sequence lists of things to do or build. Schedules are sometimes really short lists, rush lists or late lists.

Without these important base parameters, schedules are frequently more a reflection of what has historically happened, rather than what will happen. This may be OK as long as the business is fairly predictable. However it spells trouble if the product or service offering is complex or becomes more complex over time, or demand changes significantly. What we've learned over time is that improving scheduling is critical if a business wants to improve its performance. Improved performance means scheduling more aggressively (people, equipment, etc.), which invariably puts pressure on supply lines throughout the process. This is as true in the office as it is on the production floor.

THE PROBLEM WITH CORPORATE POOL TABLES

The first significant purchase made by the Carpedia partnership, about four months after starting operation and despite the protest of spouses, was a custom-made pool table. It wasn't purchased because we wanted to be hip or trendy – as became fashionable years later with the dot-com start-ups – it was because the partners really enjoyed playing pool. Roughly 20 years later, the pool table is still in head office, although it's now relegated to a basement lounge, and has been played a sum total of about five times by the partners. So what went so terribly wrong?

Two things conspired to ruin the vision of playing pool at the office late into the evening. The first was arguably inexcusable for a management consulting firm: the table didn't fit the space. It turns out that pool tables require a lot of room, and the original office was not very spacious. This should have been picked up in the design phase, but was somehow over-looked in the excitement of purchasing the table. To use the table on one side, the partners had to buy child-size pool cues, which significantly took away from the experience. This little planning error, by the people who designed Carpedia's methodology, has been quietly buried in the company archives.

The second problem was not foreseen, but makes sense in hindsight. Hanging around to play pool at the office after a long day of work wasn't nearly as much fun as playing pool at a local pub, where there were people and noise and action (not to mention that neither plan went over particularly well with spouses).

One of the many lessons we took away from this disappointing experience – and actually adopted into our projects – was the importance of thinking about the impact method changes have on the environment, rather than just focusing on the mechanical change in the process. Process changes can shift the dynamics of how people function and interact more than you sometimes realize. It was one of the reasons we introduced "prototyping," a key step in our process, so we can test a change and observe what happens in and around the process. It was well worth the cost of a custom-made pool table.

OBSERVATIONS: THE MOST USEFUL TOOL THAT MANAGERS DON'T USE

Observations are a problem-solving technique designed to get people to actually focus for a few hours on some part of a process to determine how much of a person's (or a machine's) day is adding value or not adding value. It's like being a human video recorder with the added task of having to actually analyze what you are seeing. It can be a little boring if you are watching a repetitive task, but it is remarkable what you can see if you have the patience to pay close attention to what is happening. We consistently find that as much as 50% of the time that people are "busy doing something" at work they are not actually adding any value to a product or service. It's the time people spend reworking, or fire-fighting, or expediting, or doing something because there's a breakdown somewhere else in the process. It might have to be done, and it can be hard work; it just doesn't add any value.

When we introduce the concept of observations, managers are concerned that employees will feel uncomfortable if they have a "human shadow." Employees do, of course, feel some initial awkwardness, but once they get over this (which happens quickly) they appreciate the fact that someone is trying to see the world through their eyes. Managers also think, at first, that an observation is "artificial" in some way, because surely a person being observed will be more diligent or harder working than normal. This turns out to be somewhat irrelevant. What we find when we do observations is that problems happen whether people want them to or not. Operating problems are caused when you receive the wrong information; a needed part is missing; you have to redo something; or you simply have to wait for some reason. All these problems occur whether someone is standing next to you or not. We rarely observe pure idle time, but we still see as much as half a person's day spent doing things that ideally shouldn't need to be done.

On projects we ask managers to conduct their own observations. We have found that it is important to get them to see the opportunity for themselves, rather than just relying on a consultant's opinion. Invariably managers will comment on how useful observations are. But also invariably, when we come back six months after a project ends to review the status of what was implemented during the project, we find that most managers have stopped doing them. The simple reasons they stop are because observations are time-consuming, often boring, and are not "required" activities of a manager. It's too bad. Observations are a very valuable problem-solving tool that is rarely used.

A STRATEGY NEEDS TO SOLVE A PROBLEM

One of our early clients asked us if we were interested in helping him develop a strategy for one his company's divisions. We said, "Of course." Without asking him enough questions, we drew up a proposal that laid out a fairly classical approach to developing a strategy. The proposal looked at studying the current market situation, establishing goals and objectives, and then developing specific action plans. He looked at it and then said, "Too textbook, guys. Before you go out and spend time and money analyzing the marketplace I want you to figure out what, or even if, we have a problem. If we have a problem, then we need a strategy to fix it."

Nodding in agreement, without really understanding what he was saying, we asked him to explain what he meant. He said that most strategies he'd come across in his career were too generic. "Everyone says that they want to improve customer service and employee satisfaction, reduce cost and grow. That's a basic wish list for every company on the planet. But usually not enough thought has gone into trying to figure out what the actual problem is that requires a strategy. A good strategy addresses the current gaps in the value you are bringing to the market, your ability to make money, and your organizational strengths." He carried on, explaining how he would approach developing a strategy. We listened intently, furiously making notes while at the same time trying to look slightly bored. We learned a great deal about how to make sure a strategy is a practical and useful tool, rather than a self-important document destined to be confined to the CEO's desk drawer.

The essence of what he told us is that you need to figure out the problem before you start searching for a solution. To do this, you need some sense of what your objectives are and then work backwards. Let's say a company wants to earn a 10% profit after tax in three years. If you are currently earning 5%, then you have identified the gap, or the initial problem. To close the gap, you can grow your revenue, reduce costs or both. If you think you need to grow your revenue, you can do the math and figure out by how much. If you look at your historical growth, project it out over three years and you are well below where you would need to be, then you have identified another problem. Do you add products? Change how you sell? Acquire another company? Starting with the answer allows you to put a stake in the ground and then identify the obstacles that are going to stop you from getting to where you want to be. It helps you identify what the practical problems really are. Once you understand the problems, it is much easier to craft a game plan to figure out what you are going to do about it. The strategy then becomes a working road map and a problem-solving tool that can help guide how you allocate your time and resources.

TO IMPROVE PRODUCTIVITY, IMPROVE MANAGEMENT

Peter Drucker once wrote, "The productivity of work is not the responsibility of the worker but of the manager." Over the years, we have learned to appreciate and understand what he meant. When you start in consulting, you spend a lot of time watching people work – hours upon hours of observing activities in a plant or an office, so that you can better understand how work flows through an organization. From this vantage point, you can also see the many problems that crop up through the day, and how workers and managers interact to try to fix them.

One of the most fascinating things you learn, if you spend enough time watching people work, is that the problems will happen whether or not you are there (a point we made in Lessons Learned #16). You learn that these repetitive and recurring problems eat up a significant portion of an average person's day. Finally, you also learn that the worker may have little or no personal control over the problem. The root problem often resides in some upstream department or area. Information is missing or incorrect and so starts a chain of rework or duplicated effort to try to fix the issue. Fixing errors that occur somewhere else in the process is very common in many businesses. If the upstream department needs to change what they are doing, the employee cannot influence that; only the manager can.

Of course not all errors originate outside a department. But errors are never intentional. There may be a skills issue with some employees, but this also indicates a training issue on the part of the manager. If a worker needs training to improve their skills, they need a manager to provide or orchestrate it.

Sometimes there are just too many people working for the volume of work: restaurants, hotels, retail stores and hospitals are good examples of where this easily happens. Matching supply and demand is difficult in many environments, but it is not something that an employee can control. Forecasting volume and scheduling resources to match the forecast are a manager's job.

So how do you improve the productivity of work? Only the manager has the scope of control to effect any change that will have a meaningful impact on the workload of the line employee.

THE HIDDEN COST OF A BRIEFCASE FULL OF MONEY

Over the years we've developed a well outlined performance compensation plan for all our staff, based on the actual attainment of measurable results. Not willing to leave a good thing alone, a number of years ago we came up with the idea that random financial rewards would be a novel way to recognize people's performance. To make it more interesting and colorful, we decided to give out the money in unique ways.

The first recipient was a long-term manager who had done a great job with one of our manufacturing accounts. We searched around for a silver attaché case and filled it with money. It turned out that quite a lot of money didn't look like very much when we put it in a briefcase, so we went back to the bank for smaller denominations and then layered the money with cut newspaper underneath. It looked impressive when we were finished. A couple of the senior partners invited the manager out to dinner and then asked him to come out to the parking lot, where a rental car was parked. They gave him the keys and asked him to open the trunk and remove the briefcase. He wasn't exactly sure what they were up to and was a little reticent to open the briefcase. When he did and saw all the money, he was both relieved and thrilled.

The second (and last) recipient was a consultant who had done a great job in a hospital laundry – not a very pleasant place to work. He did a tremendous job for the hospital and never complained about the difficult conditions. The partners gave him his award money in a hospital laundry bag. He was thrilled.

What was not anticipated was the reaction of everyone else in the company. No one was thrilled. One or two people may have been mildly amused at the theatrics, but the general response to both events was distinctly negative. The basic question most people had was: "What specifically did these two do to deserve this type of reward?" The choice seemed to many to be arbitrary, and it isolated individuals when they were clearly part of a larger team effort. There were even quiet murmurings of partners playing favorites, which unfortunately made the recipients targets for fairly critical peer reviews following the rewards.

The lesson learned from this experience is to be very careful when handing out rewards. For rewards to be effective, the expectations and measurement need to be very clear, so that people understand the manner in which decisions are made. People tend to be accepting and even collectively supportive if the criteria and measurement are reasonably fair. Without this, rewards can easily backfire. When it comes to handing out money, we learned that novelty doesn't trump transparency.

START WITH
THE CONCLUSION

We once heard a funny story about a lesson learned by a consultant. It was told to us by a client who himself was an ex-consultant, so we can't be sure if it really happened or is some kind of urban legend. In any case, one day a consultant was making a presentation to a number of managers, including the president of the organization. At one point, the president began to feel bored and restless. She asked the consultant to get to the point and tell her the net impact of the recommendations. Not wanting to be thrown off his agenda, the consultant replied, "Great question, but you're one step ahead of me. I will be covering that off a little later in the presentation." So the president collected her notebook, got up and walked to the door. As she was leaving, she turned briefly and said, "Someone let me know when he gets to that section."

There are a couple of lessons or maybe broader questions we can take away from this story. (1) Should you answer a direct question when asked in a presentation, knowing that you will be discussing the issue later? (2) Should you structure your presentations by answering the main question upfront and then supporting it, or should you build a case to reach an ideally obvious conclusion at the end? In our experience, these are actually interrelated questions.

Many of our senior clients are results-based individuals. It's in their nature to want to know the answer upfront and then see it supported with arguments. They do not like it when we present arguments leading up to a conclusion, because they feel slightly manipulated. They want the answer early on, so they can have a chance to balance our arguments and see if they would draw the same conclusions. So, as a general rule, we always give away the punchline upfront and then support it. In the story above, we suggest that it would be better to answer the president's question directly, even if the point will be repeated later in the presentation.

So should you always give the answer upfront? As in everything, there are some exceptions. The best advice may be to tailor your presentations to your audience. While our preference is to give the answer at the beginning, if we are presenting to an audience specific information that we know will not be well received, or we know the audience is predisposed to be hostile to our recommendations, we sometimes build the case first. In these instances, building the case gives you a chance to present a few arguments that may get the audience to at least consider the logic of why the recommendations were developed, but emotions usually trump logical arguments.

LOST IN TRANSLATION

We offer a training session about problem-solving that uses an interesting deception. In it, we present a paragraph that describes a young charismatic leader of a nation facing a tough decision. Participants have to guess whom we are describing. Given a few historical and personal details, it is very easy to conclude that it is John F. Kennedy, which everyone does halfway through the exercise. The surprise is that the correct answer is not John F. Kennedy – it's Adolf Hitler.

The exercise demonstrates our tendency to jump to conclusions too quickly and that, once we do, we exclude alternatives. Apparently our innate shortcuts help us navigate day-to-day living, but get the better of us when it comes to thinking about things analytically.

The exercise has demonstrated this point brilliantly every time we've used it, except once. We were doing some work for The Ritz-Carlton Hotel Co., when they asked us to train some of their European quality managers in Istanbul. The session was going well, then we got to the problem-solving exercise. After the paragraph was presented, a fairly bold and dramatic question appeared onscreen: "Who is this person?" The answer it provoked is remembered as one of the more confusing moments in the history of Carpedia training. While we waited, anticipating the usual wrong answer, the quality managers looked at each other a little awkwardly and said, virtually in unison, "That sounds like Adolf Hitler."

There were a few additional grumblings about whether Adolf Hitler was an appropriate leader to showcase and certainly whether "charismatic" was an appropriate descriptor. Not a single person saw the description as one of John F. Kennedy, even after it was explained how the exercise was supposed to play out. There were a couple of lessons learned from this. The first was simply to be more aware of how important personal context is for people. It was an interesting example of how regional and cultural bias affects how things are perceived. The second was to think through what you plan to present and be cognizant of potential sensitivities. The exercise works in North America because people jump to the conclusion the paragraph is about JFK, perceived to be a hero. The fact that it's about Hitler makes the error more dramatic.

WHAT DO YOU MEAN BY A "GOOD" DAY?

Golf is one of those rare sports that is often more boring to watch live than on television. But for those people who like playing golf, it is a wonderful and strangely addictive game. Trying to make par, or using the handicap system to play against others, is a big part of golf's appeal. Competition is fun for many people, even if they're only competing against themselves. However, can you imagine someone playing golf every day without a scorecard – just walking around the course, hitting the ball towards some distant flag? Yet this is exactly how many people work every single day.

When we are working in an area, we walk around and often ask people how they know if they are having a good day or not. Most people will respond something like, "I have a good day when customers [or "my manager" or "sales"] aren't giving me a hard time." What is often noticeably absent (especially in office environments) is any reference to a performance number, whether that's adhering to a specific schedule, attaining a productivity level or a service score. People often struggle to define what a good day is in any way other than anecdotes.

We have learned that many people respond well to some form of competition, perhaps especially in repetitive-task environments. They like to have clear expectations and to measure themselves. They like visual feedback boards that chart their progress throughout the day. They like to know where they stand relative to others. They like doing well. And we think a big part of it is simply adding some interest to their workday. Walking around the same golf course every day, without a scorecard, would eventually be worse than watching a round of golf live.

EVERY MANAGER
IS ABOVE AVERAGE

There is an interesting phenomenon called the "above-average effect." This is the tendency of most people to believe they are above average, despite the obvious mathematical impossibility.

There is also a theory that suggests that the less skilled you are at doing something, the more likely you are to overestimate your own performance, precisely because you don't really know how to judge it properly.

We have learned that most managers, our own company included, believe that they are better managers than they actually are. In defense of all managers, managing is extremely difficult, no matter what industry, and requires an uncommon blend of skills. Organization design and circumstance are also stacked against most of us. Perhaps the most common problem is that many managers get to where they are due to their technical proficiency, not their management skills. Another significant issue is that the key tools designed to support management, the various information systems available, usually don't support management nearly as much as they were intended.

Is this a big deal? So management is tough, and our own self-assessments are a little high. Turns out that this is a big deal if you are trying to drive up performance. A key part of most performance-improvement efforts is getting managers to change how they interact with their people: how they set expectations, follow up and coach. If managers don't see a need to change, it's very hard to get them to change.

We address this issue by doing what we call "management studies." We spend a day observing a manager and then break their time into categories. To compare what they actually do with what they think they do, we ask them at the end of the day to do their own categorization. Almost invariably managers misjudge how they spend their time. However, if you do the same study but stop every 30 minutes and briefly discuss what happened, you can relatively quickly recalibrate someone's perceptions. The study doesn't change behavior, but it does help a manager understand that there may be a better way to allocate their time, which, as mentioned, is a necessary component to broader performance improvement.

TOO MANY
GOOD IDEAS

Here's a joke we often hear: "Consultants take your watch, tell you what time it is, and then keep your watch." It's funny and, like most jokes, it's at least partially true. There is never a shortage of good ideas in the companies where we work, and we go to great lengths to find them by talking to managers and employees. So if all these good ideas exist, why don't companies just utilize them? What we've learned is that the problem is not that there is a shortage of good ideas. It's that there are too many.

In every functional area we work in, with the help of managers and employees we create a large wall-sized map that illustrates all the steps in the current process. Then we give the employees a red pen and ask them to critique the process. "What would you change if you could?" Before long the map looks like some type of contemporary art, with varying sizes and styles of critical red comments. It's the same every time. Problems creep naturally into any process, and over time they accumulate. Employees who have to deal with them every day develop ideas and work-arounds and are a good source for ideas about what could change.

The real challenge is the time it takes to sift through those ideas to determine what impact the change would have, how practical it is, and how much interfunctional co-ordination is required. Out of literally hundreds of ideas we usually end up focusing on less than 10. Sometimes we can help introduce a new method or approach, usually because we've seen it done differently in another industry. Sometimes it's just a matter of taking a good idea and physically making it work.

So, yes, we often look at someone's watch and tell them the time, but the joke goes too far when it comes to "keeping the watch." That rarely happens.

Excellent
Good
Average
Poor

DON'T ASK FOR FEEDBACK IF YOU DON'T WANT IT

So here is a lesson learned we picked up on the fly recently. Below is a pretty fair representation of an exchange between a partner and a senior manager at a casual project dinner:

> **Partner:** "So how do you like the Lessons Learned series so far?"
>
> **Senior manager** *(after a slightly awkward pause)*: "They are pretty good."
>
> **Partner:** "Your hesitation suggests you're not a big fan. What don't you like about them?"
>
> **Senior manager:** "I find them a little salesy."
>
> **Partner:** "Salesy? The whole point of them is that they aren't salesy at all. Are you even reading them?"
>
> **Senior manager:** "Hey, you asked for the feedback."

Therein lies the problem with feedback. It can be quite powerful to drive performance improvement, but it's often either a one-way exchange or a cloaked way of looking for positive reinforcement or recognition. Most managers come to realize that it's not effective to give someone feedback if the person doesn't want it. Social and organizational power imbalances also make feedback a difficult tool to use effectively, which is one of the reasons why 360-degree feedback programs often fail to live up to expectations. It's simply very difficult giving feedback to someone who has some degree of control over your compensation or employment.

If you want feedback for the intent of actually trying to improve something, there needs to be an open and honest exchange of ideas about what is good and not so good. You need a lot of clarity of intent and organizational trust for it to be effective as a performance-improvement tool.

BE CAREFUL
OF STOPE RATS

The two founding partners of Carpedia first met while working on a project in a potash mine. Each morning at 7:00 a.m., they would travel underground about 3,000 feet (roughly two times the height of the Empire State Building). Over a number of months they learned many interesting things about living underground. For example: although it was winter and icy cold on the surface, it was about 80°F in the mine. This was caused by the frictional heat created by gradually shifting earth (a somewhat unsettling fact of life in these particular soft-rock potash mines).

This is also where they learned why miners carry their sandwiches in metal lunch pails. One of the consultants on the project innocently asked this question one day after noticing that none of the consultants had metal lunch pails, while all the miners did. A burly, seasoned miner looked down at him and patiently explained that if you don't use a metal pail of some kind, the stope rats will eventually steal your lunch. A stope, incidentally, is the open space left behind after the extraction of ore in an underground mine.

So the next day the consultants all showed up with brand-new metal lunch pails (a few tried to intentionally scuff the surface to reduce the shiny glare). One of the things you learn as a consultant is to fit in. You may never be mistaken for a seasoned miner, but you also never want to be mistaken for someone who can't adapt to their environment. You try to subtly find out how to dress, how to act, and even how to speak (every industry has its own mysterious jargon). This allows you to gain both social credibility and assume a certain humility, so you can minimize the anxiety and distrust some people naturally have for "outsiders." And besides, tales of stope rats would cause anyone to adjust their daily habits.

On seeing this, the miners nearly fell over backwards laughing. It was a full two or three weeks later that the consultants learned that the miners weren't laughing at the shiny lunch pails.They were laughing because there was no such thing as "stope rats." The lesson learned? There are probably a few here, but certainly it's not a bad idea to check your facts before implementing changes.

ATTACK THE
RED TIME FIRST

When we do studies in an area, the primary purpose at the highest level is to separate the value-added time from the non-value-added time. We define non-value-added as time that a supplier spends doing something that a customer wouldn't want to pay for if he or she knew about it, such as reworking a product because it was made incorrectly the first time; or fixing errors made somewhere upstream in the process; or simply idle time when there isn't enough work to keep everybody busy. We use colors to illustrate the separation: green for the value-added time (which is "good" time); and red for the non-value-added time ("bad" time). It's a simple device that is extremely effective for making the point – except for one occasion, when a client failed to see the distinction. After a some- what confusing debate, we learned he was color-blind.

The green time is processing time. The red time is down time or "waste" in lean vernacular. Both green time and red time can be improved, but we've learned that it's harder to fix the green time. Fixing the green time means taking an existing process and reconfiguring it so that it is more productive. This is what "re-engingeering" was all about, and why it struggled to be more than just a fad that bridged TQM and Six Sigma. Re-engineering advocated starting with a blank sheet and rethinking how a process should work. The trouble with this approach is that it often leads to changes in equipment or technology, which can be expensive and is often a slow-decision process for many companies. Attacking the red time is a better place to start for a number of reasons. Attacking the red time is more immediate and means fixing some of the existing operating problems that people cope with or have to work around. Or it means tightening the scheduling of an area to better match volumes to resources, and so incur less idle or down time. The one major obstacle for fixing red time, and the chief reason much of it exists in the first place, is that many operating problems have their roots somewhere in an upstream process, which may be outside the control of the functional department with the actual problem.

But if you can get different functions working together, fixing red time is typically much more immediate, and easier to implement because it fixes problems for people.

WHAT DOES "IMPLEMENTATION" MEAN ANYWAY?

Twenty years ago, very few consulting firms wanted to implement their recommendations. This was seen as somehow "pedestrian." Since then, Y2K and various ERP system advances have pushed many IT-based consulting firms into actually implementing their IT systems. In addition, clients have become more demanding of actual measurable results. These changes have made implementation a buzzword in the consulting industry. But what exactly does "implementation" mean?

Over the past two decades, we have seen and worked with most MRP, ERP, CRM, SCM and whatever other three-letter acronym systems have been developed. Here is what we've learned: Most of the systems mentioned were cleverly designed and programmed. They were obviously developed by very smart people, who knew their particular area of expertise very well. And none of them worked the way they were designed.

All the systems mentioned are fundamentally "scheduling" systems. They are designed to help a company match and balance its resources to demand. When companies "implement" new systems, they physically install the hardware and train people to use the software. Where implementations of these kinds almost always fail is that they don't help improve scheduling. The primary reason is that they take corrupt data from the old system and "cut it over" into the new system. The issues are always the same: the standards are not trusted or up to date; infinite capacity planning is used to "cheat" the system; schedules are manually overwritten; planning parameters, such as supplier lead times, are simply system defaults; not all the necessary system components are installed, etc. All too often, the net result is a very expensive data-storage system of still-corrupt data. A potentially bigger problem is that sometimes systems, over time, "dumb down" an organization and become a mysterious black box of how the company works. People can lose sight of the original intent of the system.

So how do you define implementation? The simplest way to determine when something is actually implemented is when management use and trust the information that is provided to make day-to-day decisions on how to use their resources; the base data from which the system derives its intelligence is accurate and the conversion logic is up-to-date; managers don't have work-arounds, hot lists and separate forecasts.

NOBODY GETS THEIR MBA TO BE A SALES PERSON

One of our past clients built a dominant company in a somewhat unattractive industry by creating what was essentially a sales company. He recruited and assembled the best salespeople from the fragmented industry, paid them a lot, and relegated production to a purely supplier role.(He also taught us a few things about buying – skinning us alive in purchasing our company's services and somehow making us feel OK about the deal – but that's another lesson learned.) His simple message was that salespeople are incredibly important to an organization. They can create and sell value that has nothing to do with manufacturing cost. They fuel a company. And while they have their faults, if you ever let the balance of cost in an organization shift from the people who create revenue to the people who spend revenue, you have a problem.

Treating salespeople with that kind of genuine reverence is hardly universal. "Sales" is often seen as a poor cousin to other more glamorous aspects of business. We have a continual stream of MBAs come through our recruiting channels, and we invest a great deal of time interviewing them. Not one of them has ever bragged about their ability to sell. Marketing maybe, but not selling. We hear all about people's accumulated skills in counting money, trading money and investing money, but very little about generating money.

So while we may not have entirely understood our client's actions many years ago, we have certainly come to appreciate the value of people who help create revenue. And we have also observed that as people progress in our business and in many of our clients' companies, the ability to sell, or persuade others, becomes an increasingly critical capability.

THE PROBLEM WITH INDUSTRY EXPERTS

American psychologist Abraham Maslow was an optimist, famous for his hierarchy of needs. He is also credited with the phrase: "If all you have is a hammer, everything looks like a nail." That's a little how we feel about industry experts (even though there are a number of industries where we claim to be experts).

Industry expertise is sometimes needed to help solve technical problems when that expertise is not resident within the company, but for general change management it can actually be a hindrance. Industry experience is more impressive from a marketing perspective than it is from a practical operating perspective. A long list of relevant experience and familiarity with local industry jargon are understandably comforting to people who have to decide whether or not to trust you to help them. But expertise is a double-edged sword. It is sometimes worse than coming in with no preconceived notions and an open mind about both what could be the root problems and viable solutions. Once your expertise allows you to start jumping to conclusions without considering the facts, you're in trouble. We've learned that if our consultants work too long for one client, they start to lose their objectivity. They begin to rationalize why something can't be done even before they have properly analyzed the situation.

The reason is reflected in Maslow's thinking. As you become more familiar with any subject matter, you are apt to cut corners, whether you are aware of it or not. Experts have a tendency to treat problems they come across as the same or similar to ones they have encountered in the past. This in itself is not necessarily bad. Sometimes problems are similar, and certainly history has a way of repeating itself, but we've learned that problems are very much context specific. And usually the biggest single context variable is people. The makeup and style of management can be radically different from one location to another, even though the process and systems may be virtually identical. We work in many businesses that intentionally replicate their management systems and business processes to support their scale (e.g., hotels, wineries and distribution centers). The toughest thing for them (and us) is to manage through the variances, between locations, in how people work together and interact. This usually has little to do with the industry.

ADDITION IS EASIER THAN SUBTRACTION

It is a lot easier to add cost when times are good than it is to reduce cost when times are bad. This may be one of the more obvious lessons in this series, but nonetheless we relearned this one, as many companies did, during the most recent economic decline.

Adding cost, whether people, equipment or marketing, is generally all positive. Taking cost away, such as reducing staff, shutting down plants or offices – virtually every effort companies make to conserve cash – is almost always negative. Many discretionary costs that companies build into their infrastructure are originally intended to be perks, e.g., incentive trips, company events, even something as simple as office coffee. Perks become entitlements quite quickly, so even these costs are difficult to claw back.

The best companies we work for manage their costs against revenue very diligently in both good times and bad. They pay close attention to how overhead expenses (and other non-revenue-generating costs) move in relation to revenue, as these are usually the first tell-tale signs that something is out of alignment. They are also careful to only provide perks that have real value to people and that meaningfully differentiate the company.

But even the best companies struggle to react in time to any prolonged downturn, often because of the tendency of managers to create "hockey stick" forecasts (an extended downward revenue trend suddenly goes upward). The expectation and hope that things will soon turn around can stop managers from making what in hindsight look like obvious decisions. When managers do react, they relearn how tough it is to take cost out of a system.

DON'T SEND
BACK
THE HEINEKEN

After a successful project at a large regional hospital, the Carpedia team went out to celebrate at a local restaurant. As we sat down for dinner, one of the partners left to answer a phone call and missed the drinks order. A Heineken was ordered for him in his absence. When he returned to the table, the server asked him if the Heineken would be OK. The partner replied that if it wasn't any trouble he'd prefer a Stella. The server said, "No problem," and left. This started a fairly heated debate about whether or not there was a taste difference between a Heineken and a Stella, and even if so would someone be able to tell which was which? Most of the team thought they could. The discussion zeroed in on whether perceptions can overpower facts. Unable to leave this unsolved enigma alone, a blind taste test was determined to be the only reasonable course of action.

Five beers were selected for their relative similarity: Heineken, Stella

Artois, Alexander Keith's, Moosehead and Beck's. All five were poured into small unmarked glasses. Three people volunteered to take the taste test and were asked to list their beer choices in order from favorite to least favorite and to identify the brand of each unmarked beer. The results were surprising. Out of five possible correct selections, the first participant identified none correctly; the second participant one; and the third participant none. In total there was only one correct answer in 15 attempts. Of particular note: the partner who sent back the Heineken for the Stella scored zero for five in matching the beer to the brand, and ironically chose Heineken as his favorite beer.

The lesson learned was that it's easy to make decisions, or draw conclusions, based on our perceptions. This is generally OK, because the accuracy of the answer may not be that important. However, in many business situations the right answer is important. Faulty assumptions or perceptions can stop you from identifying the true facts of a situation. It's more difficult to create solutions based on actual facts and observations. And despite the facts, it's also very hard to get people to change their behavior. To this day, our partner chooses Stella over Heineken.

THE UNFORTUNATE HABIT OF ANSWERING QUESTIONS TOO QUICKLY

Here's an example of what should be a "lesson learned" but can actually turn into a terrible habit. A client is talking to you. When she's in the middle of asking a question, you cut her off and give an answer to what you think she was asking. In our business, there are few things more disquieting than cutting off your client mid-question and then seeing her look at you in disbelief as you rattle off the wrong answer.

So why do some of us do this? This seems to be a problem more for people who like to "tell" as opposed to people who like to "ask" (different social styles). For those of us in the former camp, one explanation is that we're upended by our experience and the way our brain functions. The brain apparently likes to take shortcuts, which hampers our ability to listen. A client needs only to hint at a business problem and some of us will jump ahead to where we think the client is going and provide an answer. Only sometimes we haven't really understood the question, so we have to rapidly backtrack to repair the situation.

The problem with this habit is that when you guess right, it irritates people, and when you guess wrong, it damages your credibility. A client once offered us this tip on how to answer questions well:

- First, listen to the question – in its entirety.
- Understand the question. Understand the context and ask questions.
- Stop. A pause allows you to think about your response.
- Then, answer the question.

Of course we had to get him to write this down, because we missed half of it the first time.

DON'T FEED
THE PIGS

Several years ago we worked in a factory that produced cookies and crackers, along with various other sweet and salty treats. Production scrap was sold off to local farmers and used as pig feed. The good news was that the scrap was generating a little revenue and being used for a productive purpose, and the plant was kept very clean. The bad news was the plant produced too much scrap.

The problem was that the scrap issue was cloaked by the cleanliness and didn't appear to be a cause for concern. We had seen the same thing at a heavy-equipment manufacturer (floors were spotless) and at a high-tech french-fry processing plant (sanitation was so efficient it was costing them a small fortune).

At the cookie plant, we attempted to quantify the cost of the waste and determined it was a bigger issue than it seemed. The efficiency of the clean-up program had all but eliminated visual clues, which ironically had reduced the waste problem to a non-issue. That was until the decision was made to allow the bins and scrap piles to build up. The speed at which the scrap cluttered the respective work areas quickly signalled to everybody that this was a bigger issue than anyone realized. Now that the issue had people's attention, the problem-solving and resulting improvement could follow.

This lesson learned runs somewhat counter to one of our maxims ("Fix Broken Windows") and to some of the popular "5S" philosophy, both of which are more in line with cleaning up waste immediately. The true underlying problem may have been that the magnitude and cost of the waste hadn't been properly measured and communicated to management. Waste is never that simple to quantify, because the cost basis shifts as products flow through the process and value is added along the way (this is also true with data processing). In any case, the clean environment led to a general lack of awareness. What we've learned is that sometimes there is a lot of power in letting people visually determine for themselves that there is a problem, rather than trying to convince them with spreadsheets and charts.

Hopefully the pigs found something else to eat. (Editor's note: A couple of years later, we were working at a facility situated very near to the cookie plant. We were thrilled to see the pigs seemed as portly as ever).

WHAT DO YOU DO WITH A "VARIANCE"?

When Six Sigma arrived on the management scene many years ago, it caused quite a lot of confusion for both us and our prospective clients. How was Carpedia different from Six Sigma?

One insightful client explained it to us in a way that eventually helped us improve our own methodology. He said, "You keep trying to define yourselves as an alternative to Six Sigma, but you're thinking about it wrong. Six Sigma provides a problem-solving methodology that you guys conveniently ignore. You have a good approach for giving managers tools to figure out what resources they need and then to schedule them appropriately. But what about when they don't meet their schedule? What does a manager do with a 'variance'? It's fine when you have a bunch of consultants running around with nothing to do but problem-solve, but what about when they leave? I need my managers to know how to fix problems."

It was an interesting observation, even if it was critical of our approach. Over the years we have learned that a key to sustaining results and continuous improvement is to have managers who are good at problem-solving. Well-designed management systems provide targets and identify variances, but other than that they are inert. Managers have to register the variance and then physically do something about it if anything is to change. Companies have long had variations of quality-based problem-solving methodology, but Six Sigma re-energized the approach with some useful analytical tools. So we shamelessly adopted what we thought were the best ideas and tools from Six Sigma, as we have from Lean, the theory of constraints, and various other thoughtful methodologies. The one caveat we would suggest is that often it's not that managers lack tools or methods to problem-solve, it's that they lack time or necessity.

DON'T FORGET
THE ACTUAL WORKERS

We were working for a company that made aircraft landing gear (actually the company legacy included making landing gear for Apollo space missions). One of our consultants was working in a parts-finishing area and determined that quite a few of the area flow problems had to do with the way the equipment was laid out. The workers agreed with him but had not really considered it as an option, due to the perceived expense of moving heavy equipment around. We did the cost/benefit analysis and then discussed it with the general manager. He loved the idea.

Our consultant drew up new floor plans and created colorful flow diagrams and charts showing how the flow of material would improve. We presented them to the GM. He loved them too. But then he dealt our momentum a crushing (but in hindsight necessary) blow. He said, "Did the workers have any input into these plans?" We told him that they agreed with the original findings and we had reviewed the new design with the area supervisor. He pressed us on whether or not the actual workers had any input. Somewhat sheepishly we admitted that we had not asked for their input into the revised flow plan, because they were unionized workers and we weren't sure it would be appropriate for us to involve them. He said, "It's possible that it isn't appropriate for you, but it's vital for us. Some of these guys have worked here for over 20 years. They know more about the flow of work than any of us and, most importantly, they play a critical role in our achieving any gains from the improved flow. If it was your work area, wouldn't you want to feel like you had some input into how it was rearranged?"

So we went back to the area supervisor and, working through him, involved the local workers in the new plan. They did come up with a better design and they were very appreciative of the involvement. We were appreciative of their insight.

THE DANGER
OF ASSUMPTIONS

One of our senior partners once had a sales meeting with an executive for a company headquartered in London, England. The executive had a beautiful office with a stunning view of Trafalgar Square. He ushered our partner into his office and asked him to grab a seat while he got some coffee for the two of them. The office had modern furnishings – a stark contrast to the historic building it was housed in. The desk was a simple glass table with a chair on either side. Our partner sat down and took the opportunity to absorb the magnificent view of the busy square.

The executive returned with the coffee. Our partner said, "I've been in many interesting offices, but this may be the best view I've ever seen."

The exec placed the coffee down on the table and replied, "Thanks. Now get out of my chair."

Like the part in a movie where the plot twist is revealed, all the missed clues suddenly became painfully apparent (particularly the placement of a note pad and family photograph). Our partner had made the simple assumption that the exec would have his back to the window. Precisely because of the view, this exec had chosen to face the window. The awkwardness that followed as the partner collected his things and moved to the other side of the desk probably wasn't the only reason the rest of the meeting went poorly, but it did register as one more lesson learned.

NEVER PRESENT
"NEW" IDEAS

We were working in the food and beverage area at a beautiful Ritz-Carlton resort. It was an important meeting. We were presenting method changes that had been developed with the help of the leaders of the stewarding and banquet areas. A number of the changes involved the movement of food to and from the kitchens, so the head chef was invited to the meeting. That was a good idea. Unfortunately, none of the method changes had been presented to the chef in advance. That was a bad idea.

As is fairly common when someone is presented with a new way of doing things, the chef objected to most of the method changes that were presented, at least as far as they concerned the kitchens. The objections weren't overly critical, and many in fact had been already recognized and dealt with along the way. But objections are road blocks unless they are properly and effectively handled. They derailed the flow of the meeting, and with each objection the general manager became more uneasy with the level of buy-in of his management team. A herd mentality started to develop. Suddenly objections led to more objections, which led to more discomfort around the room. The positive buy-in from the stewarding and banquets management started to dissipate.Three-quarters through the allotted meeting time, and less than halfway through the agenda, the GM politely asked us to do more work on selling the method changes and rescheduled the meeting for a later date.

This lesson learned here is similar to one of our company maxims ("Pre-present, pre-present, pre-present"). For any important meeting, the participants should be familiar with the material and not be presented with "new" ideas. This may seem a little odd, but it is in fact critical for managing change. By pre-presenting the information, you can handle objections on a one-to-one basis and either reach a resolution or modify the method change accordingly. Surprising people, even if the changes are relatively innocuous, is never effective.

THE INTRODUCTION SETS THE TONE

We were invited to make a presentation at an industry conference. We arrived in advance and checked in. Then, we were instructed to see the host, who would be introducing us onstage. After a quick "hello" he started to complain bitterly about how the previous speaker had forced him to read and reread his introduction before going onstage. He said to us, "Hey, I can appreciate professionalism, but it's not like I can't read." We commiserated, joked a little with him and handed him our own introduction.

An hour or so later, we got up in front of the audience, and as the room settled he introduced us. He mispronounced our speaker's last name and massacred the company name. Our partner could live with the personal slight, but the mispronunciation of the company name was surprisingly unbalancing and gave the presentation a slightly amateurish feel. It also did little to build the brand, which was one of the key objectives of doing the presentation in the first place.

The obvious lesson we learned was: Don't overlook the introduction when you are doing a speech or presentation. It sets the stage for both the audience and the speakers. Better to have the host complain about you, rather than the audience.

YOU CAN'T ASSESS YOUR OWN WORKLOAD

Understanding true workload is one of the most common deficiencies we see in companies and organizations across industries.

It's very hard for people to assess their own workload, perhaps particularly for people with strong mathematics backgrounds, such as engineers and accountants. A key point is that "true workload" is not a picture of how many hours you actually put in at work; it's how many hours are actually required. We once tried asking some software engineers to assess their own workload. Without exception they came back with an answer of exactly 40 hours of work per week. The problem is that "true workload" is not a picture of how many hours you physically put in at work: it's how many hours are actually required. No one works at 100%. Everyone has operating problems of some kind or another (missing information, rework, etc). World-class productivity is generally considered to be about 85%, which means in a 40-hour workweek you have about 34 hours of work.

And that's "world class." Many people work at productivity levels closer to 60%, which means their true workload is only about 24 hours. It's understandably hard for people to assess their own workload and come up with only 24 hours in a 40-hour week.

The reason, of course, is that people see workload analysis as an indictment of their work ethic. While understandable, this simply isn't true. People can work very hard and still be only about 60% productive. But if you are genuinely trying to improve the performance of a function, it's virtually impossible to do so without some kind of assessment of the work that needs to be done in order to achieve certain outcomes. If you intentionally, or unintentionally, inflate the current workload, all you're really doing is hiding operating problems – exactly the things you are trying to uncover and eliminate.

One of the ways we've learned to assess workload is to depersonalize the analysis. You aren't actually interested in an individual's workload; you're interested in the work requirements of an entire process. Also, sometimes understanding workload is less important than understanding the effectiveness of the process. For example, you could increase the productivity of a salesperson by requiring them to go to more meetings, but it wouldn't be useful if the meetings were with the wrong type of company.

No one likes their workload being assessed, but to improve performance it is, unfortunately, a critical step.

ALWAYS
NEGOTIATE
PRICE LAST

The temptation to negotiate price is big, but after roughly 20 years and hundreds of project proposals, we've learned that it is a cardinal mistake to negotiate price too early in the sales process. In almost every transaction, a buyer first has to weigh the product's benefits against the consequences to determine whether a purchase is necessary, and finally whether it is affordable. If you negotiate price before a buyer has decided that they need the product, you will give away a price concession too quickly.

Most proposals, wins included, are rife with complications and objections – objections that more often than not have nothing to do with price. Strangely, sales executives almost universally have a reflex that can't be suppressed: they can't help but tinker with the price to make a sale more attractive. It doesn't work. When we introduce price too early in the close of the sale, we introduce two possibilities.

1. It is quite possible that the real objections to a positive result will remain hidden, resulting in an unfavorable decision.
2. If we are required to handle additional objections afterward, there is often a second price negotiation that eats up important profit.

This is a lesson taught to us by many clients over the years (over and over and over). We expect a negotiation of price, as it is generally good business practice to do so, but if we negotiate an acceptable price and lose an opportunity or negotiate a price twice on the same opportunity, we know we've just been taught the lesson again.

If you find yourself in the sales process and the thought of price negotiation comes to mind, ask yourself whether you have handled all your customer's issues EXCEPT price before you proceed. Then ask your customer the same question. Then proceed.

HOW TO MAKE INTERNAL PERFORMANCE IMPROVEMENT GROUPS SUCCEED

We are often asked by our clients to help build their internal performance improvement (PI) groups. The concept of developing internal skills to reduce their reliance on high-cost consultants is appealing to many companies. We always tell our clients that the most important lesson we have learned about these groups is that if you want them to be successful, you have to make them accountable. This may sound obvious, but it's not. As a result, most groups have a limited shelf life. When times get tough and executives are looking for costs that can be cut out quickly, an internal group that isn't obviously accountable is a pretty easy target. We have seen this history repeat itself many times over with quality specialists, re-engineering teams, and more recently Six Sigma and Lean groups.

The reason is because many internal groups simply aren't truly "accountable." We define being accountable for a PI group fairly simply: the group needs to improve the company's profits by some magnitude greater than its total cost to operate (salaries, office, travel costs, etc). This is much harder to quantify than you might think. First, the cost to operate these groups is often higher than many realize (which is why they are periodically an appealing target). Second, many projects have measurable outcomes, but the link between the outcome and how it affects a company's profits is not always easy to calculate. You may improve customer satisfaction by answering calls on the first ring, for example, but how does this actually improve profits?

But as difficult as it is sometimes to determine cause and affect, if the internal PI group does not figure out how to make these correlations, or choose projects that have a more obvious connection to profits, the group will eventually become part of their CEO's cost-reduction project.

WHAT'S THE REAL PROBLEM?

An auto-parts supplier who made plastic components for a large car manufacturer needed to increase the throughput of one of its production lines, because the line was losing money. After studying the production line, we helped the company implement a number of method changes, resulting in a 30% increase in throughput. The client was thrilled, at least until the financial results started getting worse, not better. A thorough financial review subsequently determined that the company lost money on each and every part it shipped, so increasing throughput simply made them lose more money, faster.

The obvious lesson learned here was to understand the problem first. We knew the production line was not profitable, but we jumped to the conclusion that increasing throughput (and the productivity of the workers and equipment) would make the line profitable. We didn't properly understand why the line was losing money. Productivity was part of the problem, but not the most significant part. The real problem was actually a currency issue. The supplier paid most of its costs in one currency and was compensated in another. The exchange rates had fluctuated significantly since the contract was awarded, eliminating what were already thin margins. Increasing productivity is never a bad idea, but had we better understood the nature of this particular problem from the outset, it would have changed the direction of our analysis, and better addressed the complexity of the problem.

OPERATIONS HAS TO OWN THE PROJECT

We worked for a number of years for a company known worldwide for its quality and service. We worked jointly with their quality team and built a management approach for a number of their functional areas. While the projects were successful in achieving results, the management approach, in its intended form, didn't sustain. The key reason was that it was a quality initiative, not an operations initiative. Operations management was involved throughout the projects, but they were not the ones driving them, or selecting the next areas, or presenting the results to the executive committee. It was also considered a "nice to have" if the busy regional VPs attended key project milestone meetings. These were all mistakes.

Many companies have corporate-improvement teams of one kind or another, such as quality or Lean or Six Sigma or some combination. And sometimes they bring in outside consultants to serve a similar role.

Whether internal or external, if the improvement initiative is not owned and championed by management within operations, it's very tough to sustain. Consultants and internal improvement groups can be periodically useful catalysts to help operations management achieve their objectives, but they should always be subordinate.

TWO WAYS TO IMPROVE PRODUCTIVITY IN VARIABLE ENVIRONMENTS

Lasting productivity gains in highly variable work environments can be elusive. Highly variable environments are those where the work volume fluctuates throughout the day, week, month or even throughout the year. Typical industries with big volume fluctuations include hotels, restaurants and retail, but you also see them in functional areas, such as accounting, where the volume of work peaks at month-end or year-end, as companies close their books. We have created method changes in these environments that made processes more effective, but were ultimately disappointing when the financial results got tallied. The reason is that making a process better in a non-peak period doesn't have a financial impact unless you remove resources. You may improve throughput, cycle time or even customer satisfaction, but if your volumes are down and your basic costs are the same, productivity actually declines.

We've learned that the two main ways to improve productivity in these environments are to attack the peak and to creatively schedule off-peak periods. Attacking the peak simply means understanding which activities are done during the highest workload times and then trying to re-engineer them or remove some of them to off-peak periods. This reduces the peak's cost requirements and therefore lowers costs in the off-peak times as well. The second approach, creatively scheduling off-peak periods, is easier in some environments than it is in others. For example, you may be able to have split shifts at a retail store, but this may be harder to do in an accounting department. Union environments are sometimes a little less flexible this type of resource juggling. But this is where the creativity needs to come in. We have seen companies creatively use part-time resources, cross-train departments, pull in work from other areas or stagger shift times to try to balance their resources against their volume fluctuations.

When you come up against these types of volume fluctuations, it's helpful to remember to attack the peak first, then creatively schedule the off-peak periods.

ACTUALLY, YOU DO NEED TO REINVENT THE WHEEL

Despite the apparent wisdom of not trying to reinvent the wheel, we've actually learned over the years that it is vital for most businesses to do exactly that. We may be playing with semantics a little, but time and time again we've observed that the best companies we work for are those that are constantly reinventing the wheel in one way or another. For these companies, this means upgrading products, modifying services, stream-lining processes, and even continuously improving the way they manage.

We were recently conducting an internal management-training session when one of the senior partners suggested that it might be a good idea to share some analytical studies we had done very early in our company's history (in the early '90s). A few printed studies were dug up out of the company archives, and after we blew away the dust, were laid out on a conference room table. We were shocked by how primitive they looked. Much like the wheel analogy however, the basic purpose and message of the studies remained the same. However, digital technology and advanced graphical capabilities had advanced so far since the studies were put together, they now looked archaic.

Management styles and approaches have themselves gone through many wheel variations, and continue to do so – as have change-management approaches. This has been at least partly driven by new "management theories," which tend to be promoted by consulting firms and which form the basis of intellectual "products" that can be marketed and sold. If you sift through most new theories, they are generally existing theories that have been modified in some way. We don't believe there is anything fundamentally wrong with this, as each theory tries to make the "management wheel" a little more effective. We shy away from management fads simply because we find them unnecessarily limiting. There is usually some value in most "new" theories and approaches, but they need to be sifted through and thoughtfully applied to specific environments.

We never did show our current management the old study. The value we might have gained by showing that the core management concepts haven't changed was overshadowed by the desire to limit questions about the advancing age of our founding partners.

THE OFFICE CAN
LEARN FROM
THE SHOP FLOOR

When Carpedia first started, we were predominantly a manufacturing and distribution consulting firm, due to the backgrounds of our initial founders. We cold-called The Ritz-Carlton Hotel Co. one day, and the CEO passed the call over to the head of quality. Our timing wasn't great, as they had just become one of the few companies in the world to win their second Malcolm Baldrige National Quality Award. The head of quality's initial reaction was, perhaps understandably, outrage. After he warmed up to us and our approach, he realized that we might prove useful to them precisely because we weren't hoteliers. He had the insight to see that even a company known around the world for its quality could learn something from the manufacturing world. We subsequently learned a lot from him. Today our company does the majority of its work in office or "white collar" environments, whether health-care or hospitality or financial-services firms. What started with a cold call was augmented by the economic decline of manufacturing and the growth of various service industries. Throughout this shift, we have tried very hard not to forget that office environments can learn from the shop floor.

The basic principles of management don't change from industry to industry, or one environment to another. In many ways, the shop floor has been a leader in management practices. Many management fads start there and eventually migrate to service environments (lean and Six Sigma being two recent examples). This may be in part because many of these improvement methodologies are used to increase productivity and often the shop floor is the first on the target list. Or it may be simply that it is visually much easier to see what is happening on a plant floor than in an office. When you walk around a factory, you hear machines operating (or not), and you see piles of material moving (or not). You can visually see activity and backlogs. You also see charts with numbers and diagrams and daily production schedules posted on boards in front of production lines. Few of these visual clues exist in many office environments. Call centers often display real-time metrics up on the wall, but most office environments are mazes of cubicles, with people busily moving paper and hitting keyboards.

More and more office environments are adopting and adapting techniques that were pioneered on the shop floor. This includes basic, but key issues, such as how managers plan and schedule work, follow up, measure and communicate results, and continuously improve. It's a helpful and useful transition of ideas.

THE MISCONCEPTION ABOUT EMPLOYEE EMPOWERMENT

It's not as popular in management discussions as it once was, but every so often we hear someone talk about the need to empower employees. No one would ever argue that empowering employees isn't basically a good idea. The trouble is that the argument is usually made to counter why management shouldn't regularly follow up on their staff.

Following up regularly with staff is seen by some as "micro-managing." Adding to this belief: it's not uncommon to hear some industry titan reflect on their success by saying something like, "I was successful because I hired good people, and then I got out of their way." It's a good sound bite, and it may work in some circumstances, but we don't believe it is good management. In fact, you might just find out that the "good people" who were hired are exactly the ones following up regularly with their staff.

Defining employee empowerment, as some managers do, as a proxy for "getting out of their way" ignores a key role of a manager. Most operating problems that impede people's productivity during the day need management intervention of some kind to be fixed. This means that managers need to know what their people are doing and how they are progressing, at least periodically, so they can help identify when problems crop up. It's not so much a question of "getting out of their way" as it is a question of "What can managers do to help without getting in the way?"

We have conducted hundreds of thousands of hours of observations on people in their work environment, and one basic conclusion is that most of the problems that impede individual productivity are not under the control of that individual. The most common problems we see involve the flow of material or information in and out of work areas; the accuracy and timeliness of inputs; and issues that originate somewhere upstream in the process. Even with state-of-the-art training and equipment, an individual cannot easily fix any of these types of problems without the help and support of management. People will often develop creative work-arounds for recurring problems, which may get the job done but tends to make the issues invisible to managers. Even worse, the work-arounds often become the basis for formal or informal planning standards, which bury the problems deep within the system.

Employees can most effectively be empowered if managers perceive their own role not to be only as someone who monitors performance, but someone who helps remove obstacles for their staff.

THE MOST DANGEROUS KIND OF RESISTANCE

One of the interesting things we've learned is that the manager who is initially the most outspoken opponent of starting a performance-improvement program often ends up its greatest champion. The reason for this seems to be that people who are overtly outspoken share their feelings and opinions fairly easily. You know what they think and where they stand. This allows you to uncover whatever concerns they have and work together to try to overcome them. If you are successful at addressing their issues, their open nature can lead them to become just as outspoken in support of the initiative. We refer to this as "active resistance." It may seem a little threatening initially and can derail initiatives if you don't deal with it, but it's fairly normal – and it's out in the open.

A more dangerous type of resistance is the flip side of active resistance – what we call "passive resistance." Passive resistance is the resistance you get when managers (or employees) claim to support an initiative but don't really want it to succeed and quietly undermine it. Managers who are passively resisting do very little to help correct the course when you encounter the inevitable obstacles common to change programs. They may even discuss deficiencies in the new way of doing things with their employees, which breeds dissatisfaction.

Passive resistance is not the same thing as what happens when people pay lip service to new initiatives because they don't think they will last. (This can occur if an organization develops a "flavor of the month" approach to change programs.) These people don't think a program will last, but they don't try to intentionally derail it. Passive resistance is a little more sinister. Passive resistance has similar roots to active resistance. Both reflect a fairly natural concern that a change program will negatively affect the existing environment. However, passive resistance is difficult to ferret out. Because of this, you may never address the underlying concerns.

THE EMOTIONAL ROLLER COASTER

During a change program, everyone goes through a real emotional roller coaster. You tend to be a little overly optimistic at the front end, when the program is being hyped and people are excited. Then your emotions take somewhat of a nosedive as you discover it's tougher than you thought to change. Finally your spirits rebound as things actually start to improve – that is, if you have a good game plan and have both the courage and conviction to stick with it. We've learned over many years of implementing changes that to be successful you really do need courage and you really do need to commit to making it work. Every change program has its hiccups, and it's very easy to go back to the way things were. It takes genuine courage to give change a chance to work. It helps if you have lived through the change cycle a few times, because it gives you the confidence to know that things will get better. It also takes time to allow any new process or pattern of behavior to become habitual.

Two guidelines that we find quite helpful when navigating through a change program are: (1) Try to keep people from getting unrealistically optimistic or pessimistic as you go through the inevitable ups and downs. (2) Move with speed to limit the duration of the cycle. Change can be exciting and invigorating, but it requires careful management of people's emotions and expectations.

IT'S EASY TO LOSE SIGHT OF THE PURPOSE

Before this *Lessons Learned* series, we wrote *52 Maxims*. The backstory on *52 Maxims* was that we worked for The Ritz-Carlton Hotel Co. for a number of years. During that time we were introduced to their concept known as "The Basics": 18 fundamentals of service that they used as daily reminders for their staff. We had our own "Principles," but decided to copy the daily ritual and we changed the name of ours to "Maxims." We thought we were clever by coming up with 31, so it would be easy to know which maxim would be highlighted any day of any month. Over time, we found the daily review to be too repetitive, so we made it weekly and extended the logic to create 52 maxims: one for each week of the year, which we also thought was pretty clever.

During this same time, The Ritz-Carlton naturally did the opposite. They reduced the number of "The Basics" from 18 to 3 (now known as the "Three Steps of Service"). They realized that it is easier to remember and reinforce a few key concepts, rather than many. Under these three umbrella steps, they can introduce many related subideas without overwhelming their staff. So while it may not be quite as elaborate as our 52 Maxims, "Three Steps" seems a little smarter.

LEARNING THROUGH OBSERVATION

People are often curious about how we can go into such a wide variety of organizations and businesses and somehow help them improve. One advantage we have is that we tend to see similar patterns over and over across industries and even across nationalities. We often have an idea about what we are likely to observe well before we set foot in an organization. What we typically find are gaps or disconnects in the process, management operating systems and organizational behaviors. These gaps or problems are rarely identical, but the patterns are often quite similar. Furthermore, if you see a gap at one point, it becomes increasingly likely you'll see a related gap somewhere else. These gaps present potential opportunity if you can then figure out how to fix them or at least make them better.

While the patterns of gaps or disconnects tend to be quite common across industries, the solutions are often more nuanced and unique to the particular environment. This is one of the reasons it's difficult to create a generic "best practices" list and hope the ideas can be rolled out through the organization. Even without "best practice" lists, experienced managers often have a pretty good idea of what could or should be done to improve a process, but sometimes get stalled because either they may have tried it before (or something similar) and it wasn't effective, or they don't think the generic solution is applicable to their unique situation.

Our experience would suggest that these specific barriers are often overstated. However, a key to getting people to change what they're doing is to get them involved in observing their own environment, regardless of how familiar with the environment they may think they are. Observation can refresh their perspective and give them different insights into what solutions might be effective, whether or not they were attempted previously. It also helps to give them the ability to take generic solutions and properly modify them to their own environment.

IMAGE CREDITS

1	NUMBERS LIE	©iStockphoto.com/jenkahn
2	DON'T PUT DOWN YOUR AUDIENCE	©iStockphoto.com/ HAYKIRDI
3	WRENCH TIME: THE SECRET TO PERFORMANCE IMPROVEMENT	©iStockphoto.com/ChrisHepburn
4	CLIENTS DON'T CARE WHAT CONSULTANTS THINK	©iStockphoto.com/PLAINVIEW
5	THE LEAST MANAGED PART OF A BUSINESS	©iStockphoto.com/gautier075
6	TO CHANGE BEHAVIOR, CHANGE THE CONSEQUENCES	©iStockphoto.com/Alan_Lagadu
7	BENCHMARKING OTHERS RARELY HELPS	©iStockphoto.com/YinYang
8	TOO MANY REPORTS, TOO LITTLE TIME	©iStockphoto.com/studiocasper
9	INNOVATE THE PRODUCT, ENERGIZE THE ORGANIZATION	©iStockphoto.com/TommL
10	THE KEY TO CONTINUOUS IMPROVEMENT	©iStockphoto.com/SunforRise
11	WHAT YOU SAY, WHAT THEY HEAR	©iStockphoto.com/NicolasMcComber
12	AVOID EMPTY JARGON	Image Credit: DMT
13	WHY WALL MAPS TRUMP POWERPOINT DECKS	©iStockphoto.com/MarcusPhoto1
14	THE BLACK BOX OF SCHEDULING	Image Credit: DMT
15	THE PROBLEM WITH CORPORATE POOL TABLES	©iStockphoto.com/trevorhirst
16	OBSERVATIONS: THE MOST USEFUL TOOL THAT MANAGER'S DON'T USE	©iStockphoto.com/ivanastar
17	A STRATEGY NEEDS TO SOLVE A PROBLEM	©iStockphoto.com/Kalawin
18	TO IMPROVE PRODUCTIVITY, IMPROVE MANAGEMENT	©iStockphoto.com/skynesher
19	THE HIDDEN COST OF A BRIEFCASE FULL OF MONEY	©iStockphoto.com/titaniumdoughnut
20	START WITH THE CONCLUSION	©iStockphoto.com/alxpin
21	LOST IN TRANSLATION	©iStockphoto.com/scanrail
22	WHAT DO YOU MEAN BY A "GOOD" DAY?	©iStockphoto.com/golfladi
23	EVERY MANAGER'S ABOVE AVERAGE	©iStockphoto.com/ozgurdonmaz
24	TOO MANY GOOD IDEAS	©iStockphoto.com/malamus-UK
25	DON'T ASK FOR FEEDBACK IF YOU DON'T WANT IT	©iStockphoto.com/alexsl
26	BE CAREFUL OF STOPE RATS	©iStockphoto.com/wolv

27	ATTACK THE RED TIME FIRST	Image Credit: DMT
28	WHAT DOES "IMPLEMENTATION" MEAN ANYWAY?	©iStockphoto.com/Floortje
29	NOBODY GETS THEIR MBA TO BE A SALES PERSON	©iStockphoto.com/Talaj
30	THE PROBLEM WITH INDUSTRY EXPERTS	©iStockphoto.com/ssiltane
31	ADDITION IS EASIER THAN SUBTRACTION	©Thinkstockphotos.ca/124543475
32	DON'T SEND BACK THE HEINEKEN	©Thinkstockphotos.ca/100749084
33	THE UNFORTUNATE HABIT OF ANSWERING QUESTIONS TOO QUICKLY	©iStockphoto.com/TommL
34	DON'T FEED THE PIGS	©iStockphoto.com/Tsekhmister
35	WHAT DO YOU DO WITH A "VARIANCE"?	©Thinkstockphotos.ca/126503251
36	DON'T FORGET THE ACTUAL WORKERS	©iStockphoto.com/Photomorphic
37	THE DANGER OF ASSUMPTIONS	©iStockphoto.com/xxmmxx
38	NEVER PRESENT "NEW" IDEAS	©iStockphoto.com/Ljupco
39	THE INTRODUCTION SETS THE TONE	©iStockphoto.com/CrackerClips
40	YOU CAN'T ASSESS YOUR OWN WORKLOAD	©iStockphoto.com/VallarieE
41	ALWAYS NEGOTIATE PRICE LAST	©iStockphoto.com/ DNY59
42	HOW TO MAKE INTERNAL PI GROUPS SUCCEED	©iStockphoto.com/samxmeg
43	WHAT'S THE REAL PROBLEM?	©iStockphoto.com/photocanal25
44	OPERATIONS HAS TO OWN THE PROJECT	©iStockphoto.com/kycstudio
45	TWO WAYS TO IMPROVE PRODUCTIVITY IN VARIABLE ENVIRONMENTS	©iStockphoto.com/Daft_Lion_Studio
46	ACTUALLY, YOU DO NEED TO REINVENT THE WHEEL	©iStockphoto.com/PaoloGaetano
47	THE OFFICE CAN LEARN FROM THE PLANT FLOOR	©iStockphoto.com/Tigeroner
48	THE MISCONCEPTION ABOUT EMPLOYEE EMPOWERMENT	©iStockphoto.com/tsurukamedesign
49	THE MOST DANGEROUS KIND OF RESISTANCE	©iStockphoto.com/hometowncd
50	THE EMOTIONAL ROLLER COASTER	©iStockphoto.com/ZargonDesign
51	IT'S EASY TO LOSE SIGHT OF THE PURPOSE	©iStockphoto.com/Tsuji
52	LEARNING THROUGH OBSERVATION	©iStockphoto.com/EduLeite